KEVIN JOHNSON

ALVAN ADAMS

TOM CHAMBERS

SHAWN MARION

WALTER DAVIS

JASON KIDD

LEONARD ROBINSON

DAN MAJERLE

CONNIE HAWKINS

CHARLES BARKLEY

DICK VAN ARSDALE

TOM GUGLIOTTA

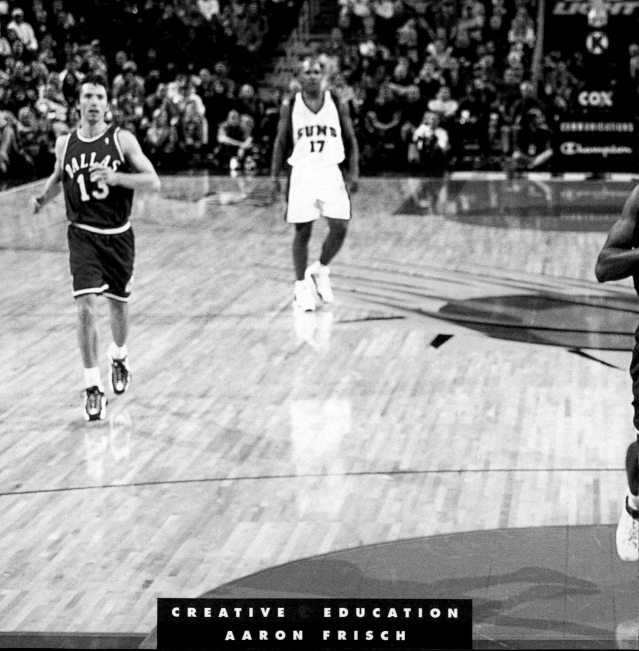

THE HISTORY OF THE PHOENIX SUNS

CREATIVE EDUCATION
AARON FRISCH

Published by Creative Education, 123 South Broad Street, Mankato, MN 56001

Creative Education is an imprint of The Creative Company.

Designed by Rita Marshall

Photos by Allsport, AP/Wide World, NBA Photos, SportsChrome

Library of Congress Cataloging-in-Publication Data

Frisch, Aaron. The history of the Phoenix Suns / by Aaron Frisch.

p. cm. — (Pro basketball today)   ISBN 1-58341-110-0

1. Phoenix Suns (Basketball team)—History—

Juvenile literature. [1. Phoenix Suns (Basketball team)—History.

2. Basketball—History.] I. Title. II. Series.

GV885.52.P47 F75 2001   796.323'64'0979173—dc21   00-047336

First Edition 9 8 7 6 5 4 3 2 1

PHOENIX, ARIZONA, IS A CITY

KNOWN FOR ITS HOT, DESERT CLIMATE.

THE SUN SHINES ABOUT 300 DAYS A YEAR IN ARIZONA,

making it a popular vacation state, especially during the winter months

when people from northern climates travel south to escape the cold.   5

Sunshine is such a natural part of life in Arizona that the region in and

around Phoenix is sometimes called the "Valley of the Sun."

Tourism is a booming business in Arizona, but the state's perma-

nent population has also soared in the last 50 years (starting at about

the time air conditioning was developed). In 1968, Arizona's first profes-

sional sports franchise—a team in the National Basketball Association

DICK VAN ARSDALE

(NBA)—also put down roots in Phoenix. Naturally, that team was named the Phoenix Suns.

{SOARING WITH "THE HAWK"} The Suns didn't shine very brightly in their first season, posting a 16–66 record behind such players as guard Gail Goodrich and forward Dick Van Arsdale. After the season, Phoenix added young center Neal Walk through the 1969 NBA Draft. More significantly, the Suns also added a great veteran player in forward Connie Hawkins.

Known as "the Hawk" for his high-flying style and long wingspan, Hawkins had been a basketball star for years—but not in the NBA. As a college player, Hawkins had been accused of fixing games (losing them on purpose so gamblers could make money). Even though he was never found guilty of any crime, the NBA banned him from the league.

JASON KIDD

"The Hawk," Connie Hawkins, was an offensive terror in the early **'70s**.

CONNIE HAWKINS

In the years that followed, Hawkins put his skills on display with

the Harlem Globetrotters and the Pittsburgh Pipers of the American

Basketball Association (ABA). After he led the Pipers to

the 1968 ABA championship and was named the league's

Most Valuable Player, the NBA grudgingly allowed him to

join the Suns.

With Hawkins on board, the second-year Suns did

the unthinkable, jumping from last place to the playoffs in just one sea-

son. Goodrich controlled the offense, Van Arsdale scored in bunches

from the outside, and forward Paul Silas gave the team inside muscle.

But it was Hawkins, an instant NBA All-Star, who led the way. "Hawkins

is a complete player," said New York Knicks coach Red Holzman. "You

have to like him, because he plays both ends of the floor. I'd hate to see

him get any better. He's too good now."

Forward
Paul Silas
snagged
almost 12
rebounds a
game for the
surging Suns
in **1969–70**.

PAUL SILAS

Like the great Connie Hawkins, guard Tony Delk attacked the rim with abandon.

TONY DELK

In 1970, Cotton Fitzsimmons took over as Phoenix's head coach. Under his leadership, the Suns posted winning records the next two

years but missed the playoffs both times. So, in 1973, Phoenix made another coaching change, hiring former college coach John MacLeod.

{ADAMS AND THE SURPRISING SUNS} The Suns struggled at first under MacLeod, but it wasn't really the coach's fault. Key players such as Van Arsdale and guard Charlie Scott battled nagging injuries, and the team also missed the services of Hawkins, who was traded to the Lakers in 1973.

In 1975, the Suns drafted a player who would turn things around again: 6-foot-9 center Alvan Adams. At first, some of Adams's teammates wondered if the lanky youngster was strong enough to man the post in the NBA. But after playing with Adams in a summer league

ALVAN ADAMS

before the 1975–76 season, Suns guard Paul Westphal knew that the

young center would be fine. "I knew from that first game that he was

good," said Westphal. "Just by the way he handled himself, how he pro-

tected the ball, how he moved so smoothly."

Adams stepped right into the Suns' starting lineup and paced the

team with 19 points and 9 rebounds per game—accomplishments that made him an All-Star as just a rookie. With the support of Westphal

and forwards Garfield Heard and Curtis Perry, Adams led Phoenix to

Seven players on the Suns' **1975–76** team posted double-digit scoring averages. the 1976 playoffs. There, the surprising Suns knocked off

the Seattle SuperSonics and the Golden State Warriors to

reach the NBA Finals.

Phoenix met the powerful Boston Celtics in the Finals.

Few fans or experts gave the young and inexperienced

Suns much of a chance, but Phoenix continued to surprise by winning

two of the first four games. Game five turned out to be a game for the

ages. In fact, many basketball historians still consider it the most exciting

game in NBA playoff history.

In that game, the teams ended regulation tied 95–95. The Suns

took the lead in overtime, but Boston guard John Havlicek hit a clutch

shot to force a second overtime. Then, after Boston took the lead, it was

PAUL WESTPHAL

Phoenix's turn for heroics. With less than two seconds left on the clock,

Heard swished a high-arcing shot from 25 feet away to force a third

overtime. After Heard's incredible shot, however, the Suns ran out of

miracles, and the Celtics won the game and then the series.

{"SWEET D" AND "TRUCK"} The Suns fell back to earth

after their phenomenal run, and a mediocre season followed. In 1977,

Phoenix added another sharpshooter to its lineup: rookie swingman Walter Davis, known to fans as "Sweet D." Davis quickly made a name for himself in the NBA. In his first season, he twice went head-to-head with Philadelphia 76ers star Julius Erving, known as "Dr. J," and scored a combined 64 points. "Against Sweet D, the good Doctor looked like a horse doctor," noted *Sports Illustrated* writer Curry Kirkpatrick.

Walter Davis spent 11 seasons with Phoenix and became the team's all-time top scorer.

Davis's fine play earned him NBA Rookie of the Year honors, but the Suns weren't finished adding talent. Early in the 1978–79 season, they traded with Utah for power forward Leonard "Truck" Robinson. At 6-foot-7 and 240 pounds, Robinson was appropriately nicknamed, and he gave the team a solid scorer and tough rebounder.

In 1978–79, Davis and Robinson led the Suns to a 50–32 record. Phoenix then continued to shuffle its lineup over the next few years. In

WALTER DAVIS

Guard Kevin Johnson's lightning-quick moves made him a star in the late **'80s**.

1980, the team traded Westphal to Seattle for All-Star point guard

Dennis Johnson. Then, in 1982, Phoenix promoted young forward Larry

Nance to the starting lineup and sent Robinson to New

York for forward Maurice Lucas.

These players, along with Adams and Davis, led

Phoenix to a 41–41 record in 1983–84. Although the

record was disappointing, it was good enough to get the

team into the playoffs. The Suns made the most of the opportunity by

winning two tough playoff series against the Trail Blazers and the Jazz.

The mighty Lakers proved to be too much in the Western Conference

Finals, though, and the Suns' season came to an end.

{A SUNNY FORECAST RETURNS} Unfortunately, that was the

last good season Phoenix would enjoy for a while. Davis, Nance, and

center James Edwards all played well over the next four seasons, but the

LARRY NANCE

Suns posted a losing record every year. Coach MacLeod was fired in 1986, and the team plummeted in the standings, posting a lowly 28–54 record in 1987–88.

The 1987–88 season was Phoenix's worst in 18 years, but the news wasn't all bad. During that season, the Suns made a bold trade by sending Nance and forward Mike Sanders to Cleveland for center Mark West and rookie point guard Kevin Johnson. The trade was a risky one—swapping the All-Star Nance for an untested rookie—but it turned out to be a brilliant move.

In **1988–89**, forward Eddie Johnson helped the Suns rack up an NBA-high 118 points a game.

Johnson, called "KJ" by fans and teammates, added instant pep to the Suns' sputtering offense. In 1988–89, he used his unmatched quickness to average 20 points and 12 assists per game. "Every time he gets the ball, he has a chance to break your defense," said Chicago Bulls coach Doug Collins. Cotton Fitzsimmons, who had returned as Phoenix's head coach, could only smile at his good fortune. "Nobody in the NBA can guard this kid," he said.

Johnson was just one of many new faces in Phoenix. The Suns had overhauled their roster, adding such players as high-scoring forwards Tom Chambers and Eddie Johnson and sharpshooting guard Jeff

EDDIE JOHNSON

The Suns shined in the late **1980s** behind the offensive heroics of Tom Chambers.

TOM CHAMBERS

24

Hornacek. This new lineup led Phoenix to a 55–27 record in 1988–89,

a stunning 27-victory improvement over the previous season. Then, in

both the 1989 and 1990 playoffs, Phoenix drove as far as

the Western Conference Finals. Suddenly, the Suns were

beginning to shine again.

{THE EARLY '90s} In 1990–91, Phoenix had

another fine season. Forward Xavier McDaniel had been

added to the Suns' offensive attack, and swingman Dan Majerle boosted

the team off the bench. At 6-foot-6 and 220 pounds, Majerle could

rebound like a forward and launch three-pointers like a guard. Despite

their talent, the Suns were quickly booted from the playoffs in both

1991 and 1992.

After the 1992 loss, the Suns decided to make a major change,

sending Hornacek and two other players to Philadelphia for All-Star for-

Flamboyant strongman Charles Barkley starred in Phoenix's frontcourt for four seasons.

CHARLES BARKLEY

ward Charles Barkley. Barkley was an extraordinary player. At 6-foot-5

and 250 pounds, he seemed too short and heavy to be able to jump as

high and run as fast as he did. His great strength made him a fierce

rebounder, and the confident manner in which he carried himself had

earned him the nickname "Sir Charles."

Barkley's addition took the Suns to new heights. In his first season in Phoenix, Barkley scored 25 points and grabbed 12 rebounds per game

to earn the league's MVP award. Behind Sir Charles, the Suns went

62–20 and reached the NBA Finals at last. The Finals

pitted the Suns against the Chicago Bulls, and Barkley

against Bulls superstar Michael Jordan in a marquee

matchup. Phoenix gave the defending NBA champs a

tough battle, but Chicago won the series in six games.

Swingman Dan Majerle was a valuable defender, leading the team with 138 steals in **1992–93**.

The Suns had excellent seasons the next two years as well, but the

Houston Rockets had become the new conference powerhouse. In both

1994 and 1995, the Suns fell to center Hakeem Olajuwon and the

Rockets in the playoffs. After the Suns faded to 41–41 in 1995–96,

Barkley asked to be traded and was sent to Houston.

{KIDD KEYS A REVIVAL} Phoenix hired former Suns guard

Danny Ainge as its new head coach in 1996 and replaced Barkley with a

DAN MAJERLE

new leader: point guard Jason Kidd. In just two seasons with the Dallas

Mavericks, the 6-foot-4 Kidd had emerged as an All-Star. "He brings a lot

of flash, a lot of unselfish play, a lot of 'oohs' and 'ahhs,'"

explained Suns sharpshooter Wesley Person. "He's always

looking to pass the ball to the open guy, always looking to

set up people. . . ."

Kidd was a creative player who excelled at running the

fast break, and in 1997, Phoenix surrounded him with more speed by

bringing in athletic forwards Cliff Robinson and Antonio McDyess.

With these players added to a lineup that included Kidd, Johnson, and

shooting guard Rex Chapman, the talented Suns surged to a 56–26

mark in 1997–98.

After the season, Johnson retired, and McDyess abruptly left town

as a free agent. But the Suns didn't miss a beat, quickly signing free

REX CHAPMAN

agent forward Tom Gugliotta. Gugliotta wasn't as powerful as McDyess, but he made up for it with superior shooting and ball-handling skills.

"You have to love Googs's game," said Kidd. "We like to play up-tempo and get good ball movement, so we need big people who are comfortable with the ball in their hands the way he is."

In 1998–99, Kidd led the NBA with 11 assists per game, and Gugliotta netted a team-high 17 points per game. The Suns then made another big trade, acquiring guard Penny Hardaway from the Orlando Magic. Like Kidd, Hardaway was an oversized point guard who could do it all: score, pass, rebound, and defend. Under new head coach Scott Skiles—and with the help of outstanding rookie forward Shawn Marion—this dynamic guard duo led the Suns to a 53–29 record and the second round of the 2000 playoffs.

In **1998–99**, Cliff Robinson helped Phoenix make the playoffs for the 11th straight season.

CLIFF ROBINSON

Forward
Shawn Marion
thrilled fans
with his
above-the-rim
style of play.

SHAWN MARION

Tom Gugliotta led a fast and talented Phoenix front-court lineup in **2000–01**.

TOM GUGLIOTTA

For more than 30 years, the Suns have been making winters even

hotter than usual in Phoenix. During those years, Phoenicians have

enjoyed the performances of a number of exciting players, yet the team

continues to seek its first NBA championship. Today's Suns are deter-

mined to capture that elusive title at last, a feat sure to brighten the

Valley of the Sun even more.